A Great Day in the City

by Casey Eggers

HAMPTON-BROWN

Look at this big city!
Look at all the buildings.

Go, jet, go!
Take us to the city.

Look at this airport. Look at all the people coming. Look at all the people going.

Come on, Mom, come on!
Let's get the bags and go
into the city.

Look at all the hills in this very
pretty city. Hills go up, and hills go
down all around this city.

Quick, Mom, quick!
Let's ride up and down and all
around the city.

Look at all the things to eat. Did
you ever smell so many smells?

Wait, Mom, wait!
Let's eat lunch right here
in the city.

Look at all the pretty shops!
Did you ever see so many things?

Look at this, Mom. Look at that.
Let's buy some gifts in the shops
around the city.

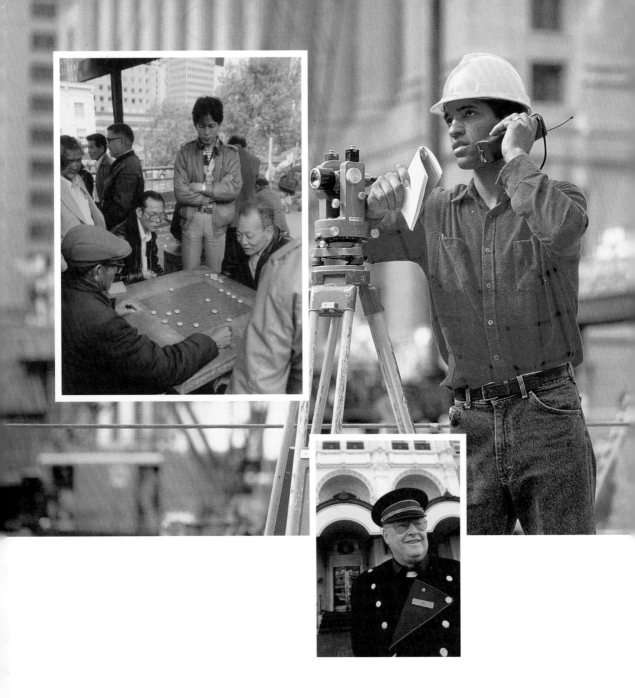

Look at all the people. Some are
working. Some are playing.

Wave, Mom, wave to all the people
in the city.

Look at all the pretty lights! Do you see how bright they shine?

We have seen so many sights.
We have done so many things.
What a great day in the city!

Oh, Mom. What a . . . great . . .
day . . . in . . . the . . . z-z-z-z-z-z.